Decorative Tile Designs
Coloring Book

Marty Noble

Dover Publications, Inc.
Mineola, New York

Note

Geometric designs and floral motifs are ready for you to color in this exquisite collection of decorative tiles adapted from rare nineteenth- and early-twentieth-century manufacturers' catalogs. They were first used in the Middle East approximately 7,000 years ago as one of the products of earthenware pottery, and gradually spread throughout the region into the countries of the southern Mediterranean. The earliest tiles were used as flooring material—especially in cathedrals, other institutional buildings, and estates of the very wealthy. By the end of the fifteenth century, the use and manufacture of this architectural enhancement began to expand throughout the rest of Europe. The production of decorative tiles has always been a labor-intensive process, and remains so today even in this era of mass-production.

For this coloring book we have included some classic Spanish designs, some Islamic works of art from Central Asia, and an assortment of motifs popular during the Victorian and Edwardian eras. Choose your own colors or follow the color scheme suggested by the illustrations on the covers for hours of coloring fun.

Copyright

Copyright © 2006 by Dover Publications, Inc.
All rights reserved.

Bibliographical Note

Decorative Tile Designs Coloring Book is a new work, first published by Dover Publications, Inc., in 2006.

DOVER *Pictorial Archive* SERIES

This book belongs to the Dover Pictorial Archive Series. You may use the designs and illustrations for graphics and crafts applications, free and without special permission, provided that you include no more than four in the same publication or project. (For permission for additional use, please write to Permissions Department, Dover Publications, Inc., 31 East 2nd Street, Mineola, N.Y. 11501.)

However, republication or reproduction of any illustration by any other graphic service, whether it be in a book or in any other design resource, is strictly prohibited.

International Standard Book Number: 0-486-45195-X

Manufactured in the United States of America
Dover Publications, Inc., 31 East 2nd Street, Mineola, N.Y. 11501

7

9

17